Sleeper

Sleeper

Jo Colley

Smokestack Books
1 Lake Terrace, Grewelthorpe, Ripon HG4 3BU
e-mail: info@smokestack-books.co.uk
www.smokestack-books.co.uk

ISBN 9781916139213

Smokestack Books
is represented by
Inpress Ltd

'I am invisible, understand,
simply because people
refuse to see me.'

Ralph Ellison,
Invisible Man

'Didn't anybody tell you how to
gracefully disappear in a room?'

Mat Berringer

'...men go without saying.
And women don't get said at all.'

Caroline Criado-Perez,
Invisible Woman

'You might say I was fated to be a writer –
either that, or a con-artist or a spy
or some other kind of criminal –
because I was endowed at birth
with a double identity.'

Margaret Atwood,
Negotiating with the Dead

Contents

Preface

The Cambridge Spies: Kim Philby, Guy Burgess, Donald Maclean, Anthony Blunt, John Cairncross. Glamorous, privileged, ungrateful. Their story has been told in many ways: as history, as polemic, as myth. The contradictions: embedded in the upper echelons of the country they betrayed, using their privilege as a means to serve an opposing ideology. Their youthful idealism, their sense of entitlement. Ultimately, their class protected them when their secrets were exposed. No executions, no jail sentences. Their defection went unopposed, to spare embarrassment. Philby, Burgess and Maclean all died in the Soviet Union, effectively swept under the red carpet.

Hiding in plain sight is always the most effective way of not being seen. Spies, writers, women. We wear a smiling mask, speak in invisible ink, turn up the collars of our raincoats. You'll never find us.

The
Apostles

The Ruling Class

Nanny. Turtle soup. Nursery. Drawing Room. Estate. Boarder.
Cloisters. Dormitory. Michaelmas Term. Arcane uniform. Voice,
and mouth. Bones. Willed blindness. Selective deafness. Around
them, servants they have turned into statues, robots.
Ornamental gardens. Red setters. Guns. Riding to hounds. Up
to town. Club. Tie. People. Ranks, closing of. Unmentionable
wealth. Landscape paintings. Furniture. Whiteness. Maleness.
Power.

Class War

Iconic, back lit, your silhouettes are history
symbolic of a war that never ends. You
have the family silver, the crown jewels,
and every acre of this land at your command.
You believe – God put you here to rule, to conquer,
and to bask in His glory. We say – the life
of the mind – ideas have no master. We say –
one day – justice will prevail, the people
will rise up, and all this will change.

Barbarians

You raise your children at a distance. Babies
turned to men before their time, exposed
like Spartans to wild beasts, cold, arcane
rituals and games. On these killing fields,
your offspring live or die, armour themselves
for a life defended against compassion.
The rewards are many, if you survive. Power,
wealth, a lifelong membership of an exclusive club.
Only at ease among your own kind, you swing,
swing together, with our bodies between your knees.

Boys

Boys. Grey serge short trousers, miniature jackets, caps.
These are small boys. But some of them will already be bigger, on their way to captain the Rugby Team, the Cricket Team, to being Conservative Cabinet ministers, to joining esoteric orders and societies which ensure they and theirs continue to rule and control everything that happens in this sceptered isle. Already they know this: it's in their corpuscles.

Boys. The smell of boys: feet, fart and sweat. Later, testosterone. The muscle surfacing through puppy fat, hardening. The thunk of dropping testicles. The gasp of mass masturbatory rites of passage, of toilets flushing over the upturned heads of the smaller, less fortunate ones. Cruelty and adoration, pain and pleasure, the twin peaks of learning to be a man. Chinese burns, floggings, wet towels, the hurling of possessions and items of clothing. How on earth do you survive without nanny?

Donald's Duty

In a long tradition, like wearing a kilt
for ceremonial occasions, or being queer
at public school, the ideology of non-
conformity is your birth right. Unlike
your comrades, you have no fat pillow
of wealth to fall back on. Follow your
conscience, boy, your father said. Which
you did, all the way through Cambridge,
as the fascists rose across the channel.
Only one bulwark against this stain,
the great ideal: from each, according
to their ability, to each according
to their need. Rugby playing Donald,
Philby brought you to this new world
where your metal would be tested.
Secrecy, naivety, idealism: this package.

The packages: each evening, the daily stash
handed over. You and Kitty in the apartment,
alternate fucking and photography, she
indulges your inexperience, helps you
focus. You accelerate upwards, a trusted
civil servant, marry well and keep the faith.
Something in the double life unhinges you.
Your handlers disappear, and are replaced.

Nobody suspects you.

Top Drawer

The men in their clubs: Eton, Cambridge, The Reform Club, places so thick with the dead cells of the English upper classes others would suffocate, the weathered leather result of the pressure of aristocratic bums, the subservient waiters and their discretion (so much discretion): anybody working class required to be invisible apart from those moments when you fuck them in a public toilet or secretly fall in love with them and accommodate them in a locked chamber of your life. You drink whisky and soda and eat tribal food: meaty and blood soaked and then white and yellow sweet things, then cheese with port and rituals that nobody knows the origin of but that cement you, make you all members of the same club. The mystery of your lives, the clothes, the suits and the dress suits and the shiny uniforms and the feathered hats and the epaulettes to make you look bigger and more powerful that you already are. What do you care about the proletariat? When do you ever meet them or spend any time in their company? What would they think of you: queer pouf toff nob? Hunger strikers are a blur of sharp-faced cap wearing men, older by far at 30 than you will ever be. You are schoolboys regressing into booze, fuelled by boy's own adventures and even though you scatter wives and children along the way, still you are not men, even though you send other men to their deaths, still you are not men, even though you do your best for Comrade Stalin, still you are not men.

Redaction I

Faded, Brue ruminated aloud.

'I'm afraid it is material. Colonel Grigori Borisovich Karpov is a relative,' he complained in German.

'He must play both sides of the net,' Annabel said, to answer the gentleman's question.

'God is great. I need an answer. Colonel Karpov is dead, it appears. He is in hell and will remain in hell for all eternity. Your patronymic is presumably Grigorevich?'

'I was his Ivan,' Brue suggested, in the sort of cheery tone he might have used at a cocktail party.

Guy Remembers Jack Hewit

Jack looks at you from the corner of the bar
and immediately, your interest is piqued.
He's a worker, surely, but not your average
bit of rough. You can tell he offers more:
which turns out to be kindness, a basic
Geordie warmth that keeps you on an even keel,
a counterbalance to alcoholic disorder.
You, committed to the struggle, whilst he
sees socialism as yet another privilege,
one that wouldn't last five minutes
in a Gateshead slum. Howay, he'd say. You
Tony Boys are soft as clarts. Not that soft,
you'd say, pulling him to you. When everything
came down and there was only flight, he was
the one you thought about, after your mother.
You knew he'd be alright, he'd get through. Jack,
as usual, left to clean up the mess.

Kim Discovers the Internationale

The Eton Boat song and *nothing in life shall sever the chain that is round us now* gradually gives way to the Internationale: *Comrades! Come rally!* Now is the time and place! Heroic figures, men marching, a red flag flying and you follow, you add your feet to theirs, patrician sole in step with the proletariat. It is your historical destiny to march, like the figures in the poster, black outlined, strong-jawed figures, your comrades. Never more than outlined images until one day you find yourself standing in line with them for bread, in the snow. This is the reward for your sacrifice, the honour of the Soviet Union bread queue. You who only ever shopped at Harrods, at Fortnum and Mason's. Now, vodka and black bread and soup until you die. *This is the time, this is the place.*

Redaction II

Either way, this was off schedule. He knew there was no avoiding going through with it. He had needed to come here, needed answers to the questions about her bracelet. So how had she lost it? Yet, seeing her now, the questions seemed obsolete. Her timidity. The shadow of their happiness. It was over.

Burgess in Bolshaya Pirogovskaya

Flatulence follows you to the Moscow flat,
its four square walls. And here you are,
the bent boozer bugared, your insides
so battered you have to accept, throwing up
is normal, part of the order of the day,
although the blood is troubling.

Gone, the boy who ran naked through
Granchester Meadows, swam in the Cam,
compact body pink with privilege. Now
you stagger slant through Gorky Park, nothing
working as it should. You don't complain: that's
not your style. Besides, you know none of it

will last, try to be stoic, accept the diversion
of the dream, a paradise lost. A country lost.
You try to be philosophical.

Redaction III

On the appointed hour, Max approached The Evergreens.
Inside, he was greeted by Bret, his difficult wife clinging to his
arm. She was beyond reasoning, her mind lost, the heat of her
insanity consuming even the firebreak of her love for her only
child. This presented a security risk. Max hesitated. A cruel
twist, of fate or knife, he pondered? A dip into new territory.

Was the Queen Told?

If I could take myself back, perhaps
it would be to the lecture hall
in the Fine Art building, 1975
and listen to a calm, clever voice
explain post impressionism,
or cubism, the darkened room
lit by images brought to life:
Moholy-Nagy. Matisse. Monet.

This hour each week was like
a poultice on the open wound
of my alienation, my wrong
footed scurry through the world
of academe. How the voice joined up
the bigger things: history, politics,
the great movements of thought
that shaped the world. I sat

in the dark, stunned, in love with
ideas, their power revealed in each
uncovered layer. So when I read
of Blunt, the minds he touched,
his mannered cleverness, I weigh
this against his snobbery, his
Queen Mum teas. I force myself
to imagine that he cared about

injustice, about class war, about
the lives of those he never met or knew.
I try to ignore the mission to retrieve
those letters the Duke of Windsor wrote
to Adolf Hitler. Marxism in the abstract,
a subject mastered, not a code to live by,
not a way to change the world. It took
a grocer's daughter to call him out.

The Wives of
Kim Philby

The View of History

is that the Bolshevik threat was more serious than the Nazi threat and that Jewish refugees from Germany were suspicious – Jewish people, known Bolshevik sympathisers the lot of them. Meanwhile they did not notice the Cambridge spies beavering away at the secret documents and sending them to Moscow. The view of history is that communism is more dangerous than fascism. The view of history is his story: women are useful in extracting information using their feminine wiles. The Bolsheviks say women are useful as wives and mothers. Women, particularly Jewish women, cannot be true comrades. They cannot be counted on, they are unreliable, they have mood swings, they are subject to psychiatric disorders.

Litzi Friedmann

You meet her in Latschkagasse 9,
amid the heat of anti-fascist action.
A comrade, brave and true, her fire
burns away your upper-class inertia,
lights your way into history. This
is your one and only barricade. As you
step forward, she steps back: for
historical necessity, the choice that
must be made. She will not be bought
by either side, never loses faith
in the bright, impossible dream.

Aileen Furse

1: Aileen at Work

She glides the aisles of Marks and Sparks invisible, seeing but not being seen. Aileen, your home counties skirt and Betjeman blouse are a uniform for obscurity, an understated version of the trilby and the belted mac. Around you, the new fabrics: nylon, tricell, acrilon. Your eyes slide across their synthetic sheen, no snags on their patina, as you clock the hand that slips the skirt into the bag. You can tell the ones most likely to, spot them across a busy counter, then follow like a ghost all the way to the Marble Arch door. Your manicured hand on an anxious shoulder. 'Excuse me, madam. I have reason to believe...'

2: Aileen and Kim

Sensible Aileen. Home Counties girl, a good judge of horses, but your judgement failed when it came to Kim, the exotic red, the dark stain on the Union Jack. The cow's lick of hair, the upper-class charm, the authentic glossy surface. Every layer of him a tribute to English self-assurance: an Empire housed in his heart, a country estate in each eye, a waft of public school dormitory as he undresses you, right down to your M and S knickers. He rides you as if you are his county mare, a champion, rosettes for nipples and an afternoon tea of a cunt, all strawberries and cream. You bear him five children like a breeder, little soldiers ready to fly the flag, if only daddy would show you how, if only mummy would stop crying.

3: Aileen in Agony

The appendix scar: you noticed it the first time you helped her lift her Marks and Spencer's slip over her apprehensive head. It was bigger than others you had seen, an angry ridge claiming the cream territory of her belly. In time, you ceased to see it, especially as the children filled this space, coming and going like flitting tenants, stretch marks deposing the scar's supremacy. And anyway, your gaze had wandered on, to younger, tauter landscapes. She slipped over the edge of your horizon, waved once or twice, then vanished with her scars, as if she'd never been. Aileen.

4: Aileen Abandoned

From M and S to Marx and Stalin. How far she has travelled. She wears his neurosis like a tricell day dress, its slippery surface inauthentic, synthetic. Drowns the insecurity with gin. He is numbers and letters. She is substance and workings. The ice in the glass. The day to day like Betty Draper. Who is she now? Only the drink in her hand makes any sense. She grips it tightly, hears the insults from a necessary distance. The friends come first. He would not risk his neck to save her: of this, she is certain. Now she has no life to lose and loses her life. He rejoices. The children are scattered like shards from a dropped tumbler.

Eleanor Brewis

I'd always known

And yet it was a shock to lose him to the storm.
His absence: as if the rain had washed him
clean away. Alone in Beirut, a sudden Kim
shaped hole in my life. Without his guidance
I learned to improvise, not tell them what I knew.
He took nothing with him, not a shirt or tie.

Those long days. Endless loop of movies in my head,
our technicolour figures on a beach. He came to me
on the cusp, the high wire act about to fail.
The game was up, before I had a chance to learn
the rules. I shelved my life, flew to a dark airstrip
to meet a man in a dark coat who spoke in his voice.

But it was not the same. He blended with the grey,
made the alien streets of Moscow a new backdrop. I
needed light, a balcony with a view of the sea,
restaurants, bouillabaisse. I shivered in my Harrods
camel coat, incongruous in the bread queue. How
love thinned in the cold. *Did you miss me when I left?*

Rufina Ivanovna Pukhova

Still a residue of charm in the folds of his face.
He is other, a foreign male lost in the bardak.
My breasts welcome him in, my only child, sucking,
sucking. Always thirsty. Hands clutch the bottle.
His ears alert to sounds beyond the reach of human:
dog ears that pick up the moan of the ceiling bug, its
theremin song. Ouija voices: wives, children, agents
on their way into the traps that he set. The medal
weighs him down, another burden. I make him
mushroom soup and pierogi, rub his back, put on
the Frank Sinatra record that he loves. We dance.
I hold him up, daughter and wife. His face on
a five Kopec stamp, like the English queen.

Brothers in Class

One of you marries his secretary: a girl
with all the right credentials, her people
neatly tucked into the top drawer.

One of you marries a Home Counties girl.
Tweed skirt, impeccable twin set, decent pearls
but in her blood an aberration, impure blue.

The secretary has the patience of a saint.
The two men talked while Elizabeth Elliott served dinner

You Weren't Expecting a Lady

He is tall and handsome and so much your junior
in years and experience. He brings chocolates,
flowers and documents. In between the essential
photography, you fuck him, Fancypants Maclean,
still wet behind the ears. In spite of all your training,
you fall in love. But you're only a cut out, have to
let him go. You'll always have Paris, and the locket
that they find around your neck, after your death.

Latvia

After thirty years of service to the proletariat,
Gypsy is tired. She wants to go home, home
to Mother Russia, and the rewards she has earned.
Her sacrifices: love, children, security. Always
in disguise, always in motion, she mates on the wing,
like a butterfly. Countries, continents, cominterns.
So many names, she no longer answers to the one
given her at birth. Gypsy sticks, suits
her wandering soul, the darkness of her eyes.
Mother Russia is suspicious, paranoid, refuses
to recognise her own child. She languishes in Latvia,
all alone. Nobody speaks any of her names.

Margaretha Geertruida 'Margreet' MacLeod

Must I wear that?

Over dressed for October. The fur collared coat
the last item not made filthy after months
of incarceration, no access to fresh water or
clean clothes, left to moither in her own dirt.

All she deserved: shameless man eater, slut,
her body a honey trap used to extract secrets
from infatuated men. Exotic dancer, courtesan,
cocotte: all these just other words for whore.

*Even as a child, she was promiscuous, knew
how to get what she wanted by pleasing men.*
Her father leaves, her husband's wedding gift
is syphilis. She endures the death of a son,

the theft of a daughter. She refuses the blindfold,
her last sartorial decision. Twelve men eye
her breasts, hoist their rifles, fire. Margarethe
on her knees, waiting for the coup de grace.

Three Turbulent Years

i.m. Ethel Rosenberg executed 19 June 1953

three turbulent years
        the state of new jersey
fear of contamination   shame

they pinned it on my parents
        Conspiracy   espionage   atomic bomb
die secure in the knowledge

I love you   mommy
        we press you close   daddy and mommy
violate human rights

all that I have come to know
        your own lives must teach you

Ethel Rosenberg called our bluff
        17th Street Manhattan   the people gathered
a great sigh went through the crowd

a collective sigh *one of ours has passed*
        like a plane going over
duck and cover due process of law

**Cold
War**

The Cold War

is black and white
with shadows
and doorways
in bomb damaged buildings
there is scrambling
over rubble
of conversations
of minds by white noise
in hidden cells
everywhere it's cold
grey
European
with hand carts
belongings
deutsche marks
roubles
there is suspicion
mistrust
all conversations occur
in code
are heavy with irony
are lipread
eyebrows are raised
tremors and tics
are expected
if not required
people disappear
reappear
in different raincoats
with different codenames
the rubble
beneath your feet
is never ever still
you are a displaced person
know your place

Winter Blue

He is speaking, the fallen man who has forced us out of the warm house into the cold afternoon. Away from the village, the light is turquoise on the snow drowned fields. We gather like ducklings, try to understand the robot voice, frozen in our navy gabardines. How one word follows another, the white breath containing stones that fall from his mouth, make a new path we must learn. His boots have carried him from another country to here, to her, to us. Now one foot replaces another, as wellingtons leave the prints of our obedient tribe. Crows sit on the bare branches of the trees, like black leaves. One note follows another in my head: I hear my mother sing Summer Time as, in another country, a bluebird hovers, garlands in its beak.

Cherophobia: an Autumn Journal

September

the table in your house
          dim light on a glass of brandy
incoherent babble, justifications

a face I know to be yours
          but folded away, cupboarded
kept for best

pond reeds striped green and yellow
          crisp, like a new shirt
fresh out of the cellophane

anger born out of fear
          reluctance to accept
a line has been crossed

on Billy Bank berries burst
          like purple beads, high
in the trees: a challenge

fork tines dislodge each bead
          into the waiting pot: you
drown them in cider vinegar

the sweet sharp smell catches
          in the back of my throat
sticks like a truth I can't swallow

I slice shallots because
          this makes you cry
juice spills all over the kitchen

alchemy: to transform berries
        and spice to dark distillation
ready for winter

this is the fourth year
        abacus of elderberries
an accounting of sorts

in the pocket of the night
        I find you
let myself be found

October

dissection and dismemberment
        like apprentice surgeons
I admire the straightness of your lines

somewhere in the thrum of minds
        silent and preoccupied
a mesh of gears, of cogs: a joining

just music and the sound of you
        putting things away in a drawer
parts of myself are reimagined

the berries on the rowan tree
        on Albert Road disappear
the birds are hungry. summer closes

time is divided into boxes on a calendar
        then in the long uneven line
of the Cleveland Hills it expands

colours of the week: pearl grey
        of early skies, gold pink sunsets
unmistakable blue of the Transporter Bridge

I sit for an infinitesimal moment
            in my own house, in my own skin
enjoy the autumn light the fading

rose bay fluff on plants dying
            back to apricot, scarlet,
a colour I can't find the words for

still sadness like a base coat
            I add to, try to cover up
soon I will see its beauty

it's not like I don't understand
            all the ways in which despair
can close a careful hand around the heart

my surprise surprises me, here
            among the opulence of dying leaves
the sudden fall into the familiar dark

November

in a garden that deepens into autumn
            the chill air sharpens, cleans
the colour vibrates its finale

dogwood, maple, hazel, birch
            a hedge dense with ivy, broom,
wild rose, rhododendron. Years are marked.

in a hot bath with candles
            I listen to David Bowie
as the sweat runs from my scalp

I think about the last kiss
            he gave his wife
the last she gave him

breathe in the corner of the room
        my back against a radiator
next door's stereo pounds the bass

life events, causes for celebration
        carry a weight, stones in my pocket
I need to remove, one by one

all week, seagulls: on fields ploughed purple,
        in laybys, cruising overhead: my father
showing me how to make it through alone

I pace the platform at Darlo Station
        hum Chelsea Hotel as a way to keep you,
can't seem to find a place to be still

stranded in a border town: no way forward
        no way back   just this lonesome bar
country music Hopper characters drink solo

but how I love the world: the bruised clouds
        trees embrace their nakedness
crows stark against a pearl sky

a feeling elusive as a fox, wayward as a butterfly
fear or happiness? fear of happiness?
at night your body across the room,
candlelit, on its way towards me.

Gateshead 1973

The cold is a killer. It lurks in the shadows, hides
on every corner with the skinny dogs. We play house
in a freezing attic off the Coatsworth Road. Hunched
in my useless London coat, I cry for spring, let
Steadmann's challah soothe my chilblained hands.
Inside, an East Yorks seam unworked, until,
at last, I leave the south behind, hack a place
for us to breathe in this resistant world. I summon up

my granny's grit, the straight-faced wit of aunties
smart as paint, their lipstick left on just smoked cigarettes.

In time, my flesh turns granite, my soul is northern rock.

Polar Vortex

Clear

The sky rings clear, a blue bell imbued
with a pale light. I tell myself I'm home,
but feel no curtained warmth, stand in a room
with furniture hidden under drying washing.
The bird in my head flutters, taps its beak
on my skull, looks out of my eyes at a storm
of radiant dust motes. Somewhere time hides
beyond my reach, pulls on rubber gloves.

East

If you look far enough to the east you will see only white: dense
blizzards, a sky like a quilt filled with feathers released into the
air. A white world we now live in, like nuns or angels. White
brings peace and a settling blankness, a silence. A stillness.
White hides everything that is underneath, erases and obliviates.
We settle for surface, the sound of the wind skimming the white
fields like a cold finger playing the bones of your spine. I see your
bones more than I did before. When the white disappears we
will see what remains. We will see what remains?

Iron

step outside and the cold clamps your face
like an iron mask, creeps beneath your clothes
into your bones makes you rigid as you brush
crumbs from the board onto the ground for
the hungry birds. How the birds are exemplars
never stopping metronomes heads and beaks
like small axes hack at the seed, fly off fly back
constant motion to survive: stop and you're done

female robin fills the ancient nest box, back
and forth with twigs and leaves day after day

only the trees stand still, spring altering inside.

Blue and White

And yes, I am still breathing. My legs still take me to the appointed place on the appointed hour. Each day starts dark and cold: the body in the bed struggles to leave the shape it's made. In the bathroom light exposes the skin tone blue against the tiles. Mirror confrontation: an agreement is made. Cold water clears the soap, the shock an ECT daily dose. In the backyard birds dissect a second breakfast, plants frost faceted, sky blinding blue and the sun fierce with January brilliance, everything braced brave against the cold.

How cold white can be: colourless sky, puffs of breath from the man on crutches. In the new café, the colour and weight of my cup. Am I losing myself? A white ghost, no sense of boundary or anchor. Adrift, a wisp of sheep's wool with no notion of the tree stump or barbed wire or bird's nest attachment. Pain bleached, a white out, when sensation overloads and cannot be borne. Or a disappearance, hidden under a dust cover, a piece of old furniture, taking a rest. Or when we played ghosts with grandma's sheets, scaring ourselves with the transformation.

Sleeper

How long has it been, this life of conscious unconsciousness? Underplayed hands, chances missed, any opportunity to shine eschewed, all in the service of a greater cause. Which has never called upon me to serve. Poised, forever on the brink, boots polished, weapons oiled and ready, body toned and agile even as it sinks beyond the horizon of middle age. Like a wallflower never asked to dance. I go home, hang my dress in the wardrobe, put my shoes back in the tissued box. Cry into my pillow.

An inconsequential job, a nondescript apartment, in a neither here nor there neighbourhood. This is my daily reality. Like Sleeping Beauty without the prince. I would have killed to die for this cause. Instead I am a ghost who has never lived. Look at my life. Do you look at my life? Can you even see it?

Sleeping with
the Enemy

Mr and Mrs Smith

In his dream, we were top assassins, a tiger and
a hidden dragon, a finely tuned professional pair,
dancing a pas de deux of death, pulling them in,
then taking them out. The perfect no frills service. Until
that bastard Chan rewrote the script, had us running
backwards towards our own demise. He figured
there was only one way to interrupt the flow: I must
finish him to stop the plot. No questions asked.
In his end is my beginning. He, kneeling, balaclava
pulled up so my Glock 9 could find the sweet spot
just behind his ear. Then the real me woke him.
He shivered like a dog, cried like a baby, told me
the details of the dream. Just before we kissed, I saw
a question in his eyes I couldn't bring myself to answer.

Cold Grey Sea

after Tennyson

We looked for seaglass on a beach I did not know
in light I could not recognise. My heart revolved
inside my ribs, a cold carcase on a butcher's hook.

Eyes down, I cased the pebbles, while you
kept silent, your switchblade tongue
slid back inside your mouth.

Alone together, we detectorised the stones,
gathered what we could: aquamarine tears,
opaque crumbs, mere fragments. Not enough

to penetrate this complicated fog. I took off
my shoes, immersed my feet in the North Sea.
The waves tried to breach the wall my head

was making, to undo with water what was built
with words. *How I would that my tongue could utter
the thoughts that arise in me.*

My America

On the coast road, Tom Petty sang of American girls
raised on promises while the sky opened like a parachute
and she felt herself caught in the path of an electrical storm.

Crackle of static from long legs, tooled boots, eyes blanked
behind shades, hair curling to the collar of his leather jacket
and the plump pout of a young Elvis.

The freefall through ice cloud, frostbite and
a chronic lack of oxygen almost finished her
but she held her nerve, let instinct guide her down.

By the time night fell, she was reclaiming her body
on the bedspread of the Musselburgh B and B,
an open window allowing the sound of the sea.

No promises and no illusions. 'Take it easy, baby,'
she said, then rode him all night, singing her siren song
until they washed up, spent, on the morning's shore.

Tainted Love

So much I've learned in your company, not always
what I wanted to know. The best make of pickups
for a homemade guitar, and how to fit them, for one:
humbucker coils, magnets and poles mansplained
until I am drenched in alien language, my head unable
to shut the door on all these facts, stuck on the wheel

of your Asperger's, as are you. You also showed me
how to tease a spider from its lair: an electric toothbrush
summoning a savage rush of limbs and pedipalps, always
unnerving. As are you, when, after breaking my window,
you scamper up an untethered ladder, rage turning the air
thick as blood. Maybe you will remember the times

you made me cry, or maybe only the times I raged
because my tears could never turn the seaweed wet.
The wine glass is not even half full, not even half empty,
but sometimes the sound of your voice soothes,
a childhood memory, a ballerina spinning slowly
under the lifted lid of the velvet box.

My Dress Hangs There

after Frida Kahlo's painting 1933

That first time, I took off my dress
Hung it on the bar above his bed.
The moon's cool face looked on
without expression, as I lay

like an effigy between the sheets,
held tight in the corset of my bones, felt
my heart's tattoo pulse just enough blood
to keep my body still.

White noise streamed to each ear
drowned out the voices whispering
'Escape' as his unfamiliar shape appeared
outlined in the doorway.

The dress quivered, a black sail,
hoisted above the crossing of the night
as his hands found the tears
in my fabric,

the unstitched seams, the missing buttons.
In the morning, I turned on my back,
watched horses paint themselves
on his window.

Gaze

chip
your primitive phone and its bleat
insinuates a chip an implant
in the back of her neck she feels
the prick like the sting of an insect
insignificant at first but
proliferation begins here

carved angel
arms reach up narrow the gap
between woman and angel
her face on the face looking down
your eye on the shape she makes
you keep your distance place her
inside the lens

scallop
tight shut the mouth of the scallop
mute before the voice of the sea
the wind tries to prise her open
inscribes defiance as
venus hides inside
covers herself with her hair

oh meine Kinder
oh my broken
the cord she cannot undo
the tug around her neck
her neck in your hands
eyes in the back of her head
eyes on the back of her head

Berlin wall
the wall she built decades before
her history buried under the ruins
camera hands first rufescent then
Prussian blue with cold
she traps time in the moment
as graffiti blurs blends into dust

you spy on my aloneness
battered in salt she makes obeisance
to the green weed a riot of spores
in awe of clinginess attachment
to stone to the being in one place
lost among others of your kind
you spy on her aloneness

battle of the gazes
at last she is subject she subjects
you to objectification points
the camera in your direction
her gaze hidden behind shades
but it's you she's looking at,
you she offers this open mouth

strive to sanctify the lost hands
hold the image the still life created
of tools of brass of metal in the cold garden
she strives to sanctify the lost hands
of maiden victims of paternal rage
hidden like snowdrops in the earth
she makes a memorial to her buried self

gaze at the indiscernible horizon
her shadow sandwiched between
the flat sands and the sea her gaze
at the indiscernible horizon
recrimination floats atop the angry waves
shakes a wet fist at the gazer who keeps
his distance hopes she will turn around

camera obscura
surveillance lens focused as if
her version might be perverse
flip bridge invert reality
subvert everything within
her gaze drag it all into
her dark and bloody chamber

mammalian encumbrance
prolonged gaze of bipeds, nostalgia
for the ocean their amphibious past
calls them to shed layers of mammalian
encumbrance unpeel the comfort of ego
reveal webbed feet permeable skin
remembered gills return themselves
to the relief of water

full fathoms five
just the edge of her rump the tip
of her hair face lost in the window
her gaze into the drowned car
the unreachable losses here in this city
where full fathoms five they all lie
and she is the only surviving witness

Over the Hills and Far Away

When you set out, you do not know
if you'll be coming back. The sheep
take up their places, stand stockstill
like furniture on a green carpet.
Their shadows stretch, finger
the hedge. You stand at the gate.

Path one is a travelogue, rolling hills
and the rational world wound by turbines.
You are Gortex, you are Rohan, layered
in reason, protected against the elements.
Impenetrable. Compass and Ordnance Survey
keep you straight and you make no deviation.

Path two is a Grimm Tale with light-
absorbing pines, camouflaged containers
and the stink of a recently scrubbed
crime scene. The half-drawn fan of a crow's wing
hangs from the lower branch of a blackthorn.
You are warned about something.

Path three is a love story. You bump
against each other over rutted tracks,
attention-seeking mud distracting you.
In the woods, the sun gets lost. You play
follow my leader, taking turns, until
the trees part to show you the way home.

Sleeping Beauty

Spindle or distaff, something had her floored:
an aversion to the domestic, sprung perhaps
from Miss Whittaker's plump digits, pulling out
her stitches one by one. She was undone.

After, she thought she was immune, vaccinated
against the wiles of Angel in the House,
free to open the door, walk her own path.
Until the prince of men arrived, pulling up

in his Ford Cortina, sea glass eyes so deep,
she was drowning before she knew. The apron
wrapped itself around her waist, tightened,
tightened. Until the prick of revelation found

its way under her fingernail, released her
from the spell: of love, of duty, who can tell?
She cut her way out with the kitchen knife,
abseiled down the ivy in her underwear,

cried a river to take her to a new shore. Now,
she claims each day, hoists her own flag,
bare feet planted on earth she tends and tills:
everything that grows here is hers.

Truth, Dare, Kiss or Promise?

Truth
a plain stranger I deny
no interest in a face
without a mask a story
told straight without twist
or turn. I prefer the subtle trail
of breadcrumbs cast
for the keen of eye
to follow if they

Dare
this barbed wire fence no
invitation upright shards of glass
catch the light cast prisms
that enchant then pierce
the bravehearts who chance it for a

Kiss
yours the awakener the soft lips
held like a chloroformed pad
steal my breath at the inhale
then resuscitate until
look at the blood it flows
through my transparent veins
a red flag, a kind of

Promise
though we both keep
our fingers crossed

Motherland

A Touch of the Vapours

'In the old days, if a woman wished to escape a difficult encounter, she could plead a case of the vapours and retire to her Victorian fainting couch.'

Darkness of drawn curtains and the remembered slights
of a long life, relived: reinvented to accentuate the pain
as if to cauterise a wound that festered over decades.
How the women come and go, their tongues quiet knives,
henbane tipped. How the men use her, repose her limbs,
cage her in the dollhouse, hide the key. She drifts around
the rooms, names the furniture, reads all the stories
in the doll library. In the empty nursery, the windows
are open. Just one child remains, his saucer eyes
swallow her. Caught in the vortex she spins and spins.
Spewed onto the sofa, she waits for him to bring
the pills and tea that keep them from the light.

My Mother as a Music Hall Favourite

The boards welcome her small feet as she
trips onto the stage, and the audience roars
in anticipation of her catch phrase – put wood
in hole! Little Jeannie! her auburn curls bounce
as she tap dances, her smile wide as Yorkshire,
her voice big enough to rouse the troops, let
Hitler know he's not welcome in these parts.

Comforter

Among the things she loved was a pink eiderdown
feather filled from long dead ducks but still
puffed enough to tuck around her reclining form
on days when even sitting up seemed more
than she could manage. After the rituals of pills,
eyedrops and tea, she made herself a nest,
became her own chick, a hatchling barely dry,
awaiting the arrival of her mother, whose
devoted beak dripped with tenderness.

Saltburn Pier with My Mother

Your feet and my feet on the weathered boards,
your arm in mine. The stick keeps you upright
in the northern breeze, while the salt air uncovers
the woman I once knew. Years and cares blown
from your face as you drink in the view, recall
all the oceans of your life, from Flamborough Head
to the Great Bitter Lakes, from the Bristol Channel
to Cardigan Bay, to both sides of the German Sea.
What you liked was the way it always changed,
that view from the beach of water on the move.
Later, landlocked, you lived like a stranded dolphin,
gasping for breath, unable to help yourself, slowly
collapsing under your own weight.

My Mother as Captain of a Grimsby Trawler

Veteran skipper of the Ross Kildare, her bandy legs
a joke until the sea rose tall as houses: her crew
soon thanked the lord that she would always
see them through. The wheelhouse queen, cap
perched on auburn beehive, with the pipe
she always smoked clamped upside down
in crimson lipsticked mouth to keep it dry.

Seeing in the Dark

She reclines, mirror and medicine in the blue bag,
the little table with half empty tea cups, the crumbs
of countless fig rolls, used tissues like dead carnations,
the ravaged blister packs she can't quite throw away.
Drops at regular intervals, her practised expertise,
one eye on her one eye in anxious self protection,
blindness a wraith that stalks her by night
and by day, its dark mists approach from every
corner of the room. Spectacles, an Ian Rankin
she has already read, the book held close,
Eschenbach to hand. The light above her pools
on the page, lets her track each familiar word,
follow the lines that guide her through, like a sailor,
feeling the ropes slide between her hands.

My Mother as a Member of the Royal Horticultural Society

Her hands, darkened by years of soil, gesture
to the team of men, their wheelbarrows sky
high with horse manure. That's right, lads, she says,
in Yorkshire posh, put it all over there. Then lapses.
There's nowt better for tomatoes, as tha knows
nowt better for the perfect Yorkshire rose.

Graeae

You hold the mirror up to your face, examine
the one good eye: its glaucous orb gazes back.
Say, Dino, when is it my turn to see what you see,
feel what you feel? Your sisters' clamour deafens.
There's a roaring in your ears like the sea caught
in a spring tide, as the moon blinds in fullness, then
begins its fade. You know it's time to pass on
this treasure, share this apocalyptic vision.
You shake the orb, wait for it to clear once more,
turn its lucent gaze back on yourself.

My Mother as Cat Woman,
the Undetected Jewel Thief

Unlikely as it seemed from her small stature
and the curvy hips, she was an expert inserter:
like a shape shifting slug, she found her way
into the smallest crack, slid through keyholes
and under doors into intimate space. There
she lifted what she could, her hands deft in
elbow length kid gloves, her diamond bright
stash slung over her perfect shoulder. No one
except me ever put her in the frame. After she died,
I encountered the gloves down the side of the sofa,
a madeleine of memory, a Proustian punch in the gut.

My Mother as Best-selling Lady Author

Her nom de plume amused her: Catherine deVille,
a frenchified affair that smacked of class and sex:
both qualities she used to infuse Petra Gray, her
flapper sleuth, whose love of crack and booze
did not detract, did not obstruct her in her quest
for truth, and for the perfect, unencumbered lay.

Ritual

Early, but the light chimes dawn prayer
and you remove your shoes, leave them on the beach
like a suicide note. Reverent entrance. Waves
grey green, white surplice, toll for you. Shock
of immersion triggers survival spasm: arms
lead legs into the ritual, repeated and repeated.
Through resistance, the weight, the effort. In search
of her face: somewhere in the window of the sea,
she will allow herself to be seen. Paralysed float,
the faded moon above, toes in front, jaunty and comic.
Every day, the same. The return to the place where
you lower your feet to the sand, feel the water
suck around your thighs, stumble to the shore.
Your shadow precedes you, the shape of a woman
who puts her shoulders back and picks up her towel.

Notes

The Apostles
The Cambridge Apostles are the most famous and mysterious secret society at Cambridge University: Blunt, Philby, Burgess and Maclean were all members. Supposedly dedicated to intellectual pursuits, the Apostles hold meetings weekly, during which one of the members delivers a prepared speech on a given topic, which is then discussed. Sardines on toast are served.

Donald's Duty
In the 1930s, Donald Maclean was recruited by the NKVD. He later joined the Diplomatic Service. Kitty Harris, a long serving Soviet agent, was his liaison from 1937. Maclean would visit Harris' flat in Bayswater after work, with documents to photograph.

Guy Remembers Jack Hewitt
A Tony boy is slang for someone who went to Eton School. It can simply mean posh. Jack 'Jacky' Hewit was born May 17, 1917 in England and died December 30, 1997. He had been a dancer and, later, a civil servant and intelligence agent. Over the course of his life Hewit had relationships with Anthony Blunt, Guy Burgess and Christopher Isherwood.

Redaction I, II and III
These poems consist of phrases randomly taken from John le Carré's novels *A Most Wanted Man* and *Spy Sinker*, using the birth and death dates of the Cambridge 5.

Latvia
Kitty Harris was an outstanding agent-courier who spoke four languages. In 16 years of service, she worked under 17 different names, under more than 40 Soviet intelligence officers, with 24 agents, one of whom was Donald Maclean.

Margaretha Geertruida 'Margreet' MacLeod
The subject of this poem is better known today as Mata Hari.

Acknowledgements

'My Dress Hangs There' was first published in *Prole*. 'Cold grey sea' first appeared on the Northern Poetry Library website. 'Saltburn Pier with My Mother' and 'Winter Blue' were first published on the Celebrating Change website. Some of these poems were first published in Jo Colley, *How to Break a Horse* (Blueprint Poetry, 2019).